DAD JOKES: 1000 OF THE BEST (AND WORST) DAD JOKES

FOR DADS WHO THINK THEY'RE FUNNY!

JOHN THOMAS

INTRODUCTION

Staring into the eyes of your first-born child is an incredible experience. Your world changes in a heartbeat and life will never be the same..."*from this day forward*" you think to yourself, "*I shall be a good dad, NO...a* great *dad. And I'll give them all the things I didn't have when I was growing up, and most of all,*" you say to yourself in a proud voice, "*most of all, I will be a funny Dad!*" and you smile to yourself while thinking of all the puns that are now available to you as a Dad.

Regardless of what people say out-loud, we all know that deep down (sometimes *really* deep down), everyone loves Dad jokes!

So we toiled away to compile this book and bring

you the absolute tip-top, pun-tastic Dad Jokes... A whopping 1,000 of them!

As is usually the case when Dad Jokes are involved, prepare yourself to laugh, to cry and to cringe in equal measure...

What do you call a fake noodle? An Impasta.

How much does a hipster weigh? An instagram.

Atheism is a non-prophet organisation.

What cheese can never be yours? Nacho cheese.

The shovel was a ground breaking invention.

What do you do with a dead chemist? You barium.

What do you call a beautiful pumpkin?
GOURDgeous.

What do you call a cow with two legs? Lean beef.

A cross eyed teacher couldn't control his pupils.

To write with a broken pencil is pointless.

How does Moses make coffee? Hebrews it.

Sausage puns are the wurst.

What's america's favorite soda? Mini soda.

What do you call a french pig? Porque.

How do trees access the internet? They log on.

Is your refrigerator running? Better go catch it.

What does a house wear? A dress.

What do you call crystal clear urine? 1080pee.

An untalented gymast walks into a bar.

Let me FILL you in on my trip to the dentist.

Models of dragons are not to scale.

What do you call a young musician? A minor.

What do you mean June is over? Julying.

Going to bed with music on gave him sound sleep.

I, for one, like Roman numerals.

How do mountains see? They peak.

This is not alcohol, water you thinking?!

The earth's rotation really makes my day.

What kind of shoes do ninjas wear? Sneakers.

I had a pun about insanity but then I lost it.

I bought a wooden whistle but it wooden whistle.

The bomb didn't want to go off. So it refused.

The sore mummy needed a Cairo-practor

On Halloween October is nearly Octover.

Pig puns are so boaring.

What does Superman have in his drink? Just ice.

When does a farmer dance? When he drops the beet.

Can February March? No, but April May.

What do you do to an open wardrobe? You closet.

A backwards poem writes inverse.

Getting the ability to fly would be so uplifting.

The soundtrack for Blackfish was orcastrated.

Where do you imprison a skeleton? In a rib cage.

Garbage collectors are rubbish drivers!

Why was dumbo sad? He felt irrelephant.

Old skiers never die. They just go down hill.

You know why I like egg puns? They crack me up!

I really look up to my tall friends.

Long fairy tales have a tendency to dragon.

It takes guts to make a sausage.

How many apples grow on a tree? All of them.

The shovel was a ground-breaking invention.

What's brown and sticky? A stick.

Why is Peter Pan always flying? He neverlands.

What's orange and sounds like a parrot? A carrot.

No I'm not insulting you, I'm describing you.

If I had a face like yours, I'd sue my parents.

You're so fake, Barbie is jealous.

I'm jealous of people that don't know you!

You, sir, are an oxygen thief!

Why don't you go play in traffic.

Please shut your mouth when you're talking to me.

I'd slap you, but that would be animal abuse.

I'm busy now. Can I ignore you some other time?

If ugly were a crime, you'd get a life sentence.

I can lose weight, but you'll always be ugly.

Shock me, say something intelligent.

There is no vaccine against stupidity.

You're like Monday mornings, nobody likes you.

All day I thought of you... I was at the zoo.

You're so fat, you could sell shade.

Don't you need a license to be that ugly?

Stupidity is not a crime so you are free to go.

You are so old, your birth-certificate expired.

You're so dumb that you got hit by a parked car.

You're so fat, you leave footprints in concrete.

Why do bananas need sunscreen? Because they peel.

RIP boiled water. You will be mist.

I hate perforated lines, they're tearable.

The rotation of earth really makes my day.

What's Forrest Gump's Facebook
password? 1forest1

What does a house wear? A dress.

Want to hear a word I just made up? Plagiarism.

Had seafood last night, now I'm eel.

How do you drown a hipster? In the mainstream.

Nostalgia isn't what it used to be.

What time is it? I don't know. It keeps changing.

How do monsters prefer their eggs? - Terrifried

Will sell broken Guitars. No strings attached.

What is the computer's favorite food? Microchips.

Toilet paper plays an important role in my life.

Velcros are just a big rip-off.

One pen to the other: You are INKredible.

The 3 unwritten rules of business: 1... 2.... 3....

What's the biggest pan in the world? - Japan.

Care to seduce a large woman? Piece of cake.

Which bees produce milk? The boo-bees!

Where does the General keep his armies?

A dyslexic man walks into a bra.

-----

2

101 - 200

What do you call bears with no ears? B

What's brown and sticky? A stick.

What's a foot long and slippery? A slipper.

How does NASA organize a party? They planet.

Cole's Law: Thinly Sliced Cabbage

Don't trust atoms, they make up everything.

R.I.P boiled water. You will be mist.

Atheism is a non-prophet organization.

I used to be addicted to soap, but I'm clean now.

Did you hear about the kidnapping at school?

It's okay. He woke up.

Don't spell part backwards. It's a trap.

I don't engage in mental combat with the unarmed.

How did I escape Iraq? Iran.

I'm glad I know sign language, it's pretty handy.

I hate peer pressure and you should too.

What do you call a cow with no legs? Ground beef.

With great reflexes comes great response ability.

When plumbers sleep do they have pipe dreams?

My math teacher called me average. How mean!

The best time to open a gift is the present.

How does Moses make his tea? Hebrews it.

How do trees access the internet? They log in.

I used to be a banker, but then I lost interest.

I wanna make a joke about sodium, but Na..

Wife: "You're addicted to skin lotion!"

Husband: "Go ahead. Rub it in my face."

I tried to catch some fog, I mist.

I hate insects puns, they really bug me.

Q: What did one ocean say to the other ocean?

A: Nothing, they just waved.

What underwear does clouds wear? Thunderwear!

I am so poor I can't even pay attention.

What is a baptized Mexican called? Bean dip.

Fishermen are reel men.

The other says, "I'm a big metal fan."

What does "reading comprehension" even mean?

I would give my right arm to be ambidextrous!

I put the "fun" in dysfunctional.

Your gene pool could use a little chlorine.

Do German cats have multiple lives? Nein.

When is a door not a door? When it's ajar.

What do ghosts serve for dessert? I Scream.

On the other hand, you have different fingers.

A: He is all right now.

What if there were no hypothetical questions?

What do people wear in a trench? Trench coats.

Why don't cannibals eat clowns? They taste funny.

A plateau is the highest form of flattery.

What do you call a fake noodle? An Impasta!

Which day do chickens hate the most? Friday.

An opinion without 3.14159 is just an onion.

What's a horse's favorite sport? Stable Tennis.

STRESSED is just DESSERTS spelled backward.

Fixing broken windows is a pane in the glass.

Student: "At the bottom of the page!"

What did the tree say to autumn? Leaf me alone.

I like using misdirection in my jokes, or do I?

Cells multiply by dividing.

What idiot called it a vet instead of a dogtor?

Password looks at itself in the mirror:

How did the reporter kill himself? Noosepaper.

Tea is like F5 to me, it's refreshing.

What nationality is Santa Claus? North Polish

Can February March? No, but April May!

A life in politics is full of parties.

What tea do hockey players drink? Penaltea!

I'd call someone pregnant "totally screwed".

Want to hear a joke about paper? Nevermind it's tearable.

Why did the cookie cry? Because his father was a wafer so long!

What do you call a belt with a watch on it? A waist of time.

How do you organize an outer space party? You planet.

I went to a seafood disco last week... and pulled a mussel.

Do you know where you can get chicken broth in bulk? The stock market.

I cut my finger chopping cheese, but I think that I may have greater problems.

My cat was just sick on the carpet, I don't think it's feline well.

Why did the octopus beat the shark in a fight? Because it was well armed.

What did daddy spider say to baby spider? You spend too much time on the web.

There's a new type of broom out, it's sweeping the nation.

What did the Buffalo say to his little boy when he dropped him off at school? Bison.

Have you ever heard of a music group called Cellophane? They mostly wrap.

Why does Superman gets invited to dinners? Because he is a Supperhero.

How was Rome split in two? With a pair of Ceasars.

A scarecrow says, "This job isn't for everyone, but hay, it's in my jeans."

A Buddhist walks up to a hot dog stand and says, "Make me one with everything."

Did you hear about the guy who lost the left side of his body? He's alright now.

What do you call a girl with one leg that's shorter than the other? Ilene.

I did a theatrical performance on puns. It was a play on words.

I bet the person who created the door knocker won a Nobel prize.

Towels can't tell jokes. They have a dry sense of humor.

Two birds are sitting on a perch and one says "Do you smell fish?"

Do you know sign language? You should learn it, it's pretty handy.

Why did one banana spy on the other? Because she was appealing.

What do you call a cow with all of its legs? High steaks.

After the accident, the juggler didn't have the balls to do it.

I used to be afraid of hurdles, but I got over it.

I read a book on anti-gravity. I couldn't put it down.

I couldn't remember how to throw a boomerang but it came back to me.

What should you do if you are cold? Stand in the corner. It's 90 degrees.

The energizer bunny went to jail. He was charged with battery.

-----

3

201 - 300

What did the alien say to the pitcher of water? Take me to your liter.

What happens when you eat too many spaghettiOs? You have a vowel movement.

The soldier who survived mustard gas and pepper spray was a seasoned veteran.

What do you call a bear with no teeth? A gummy bear.

Why shouldn't you trust atoms? They make up everything.

What's it called when you have too many aliens?
Extraterrestrials.

Want to hear a pizza joke? Nevermind, it's too
cheesy.

What do cows tell each other at bedtime? Dairy
tales.

Why can't you take inventory in Afghanistan?
Because of the tally ban.

Why didn't the lion win the race? Because he was
racing a cheetah.

What happens to nitrogen when the sun comes up?
It becomes daytrogen.

What's it called when you put a cow in an elevator?
Raising the steaks.

Why did the tomato turn red? Because it saw the
salad dressing.

What kind of car does a sheep drive? Their
SuBAHHru.

What do you call a line of rabbits marching backwards? A receding hairline.

Why don't vampires go to barbecues? They don't like steak.

Why should you never trust a train? They have loco motives.

The future, the present and the past walked into a bar. Things got a little tense.

Have you ever tried to eat a clock? It's very time consuming.

I wondered why the baseball was getting bigger. Then it hit me.

Read enough of our funny puns, and you'll be punstoppable.

Yesterday a clown held the door for me. It was a nice jester.

I used to go fishing with Skrillex but he kept

dropping the bass.

The wedding was so emotional even the cake was in tiers.

Why can't bicycles stand up on their own? Since they are 2 tired.

I owe a lot to the sidewalks. They've been keeping me off the streets for years.

Imagine if alarm clocks hit you back in the morning.It would be truly alarming.

Why is a skeleton a bad liar? You can see right through it.

What do you receive when you ask a lemon for help? Lemonaid.

A man sued an airline company after it lost his luggage. Sadly, he lost his case.

What does a dog say when he sits down on a piece of sandpaper? Ruff!

At my boxing club there is only one punch bag. I hate waiting for the punch line!

Einstein developed a theory about space, and it was about time too.

I was accused of being a plagiarist, their word not mine.

My friends say they don't like skeleton puns. I should put more backbone into them.

Why does the singer of Cheap Thrills not want us to Sia?

Traveling on a flying carpet is a rugged experience.

Cartoonist found dead in home. Details are sketchy.

The old woman who lived in a shoe wasn't the sole owner,there were strings attached.

Did you hear about the crime in the parking garage? It was wrong on so many levels.

My new diet consists of aircraft, its a bit plane.

Have you ever tried to milk a cow which has been cut in half? Udder madness.

Why are there fences on graveyards? Because people are dying to get in.

Why do trees have so many friends? They branch out.

Never discuss infinity with a mathematician, they can go on about it forever.

Why don't some couples go to the gym? Because some relationships don't work out.

Don't trust people that do acupuncture, they're back stabbers.

A persistent banker wouldn't stop hitting on me so I asked him to leave me a loan.

I ordered a book of puns last week, but i didn't get it.

People say i look better without glasses but i just can't see it.

Don't judge a meal by the look of the first course. It's very souperficial.

I heard Donald Trump is going to ban shredded cheese, and make America grate again.

I relish the fact that you've mustard the strength to ketchup to me.

Police were called to a daycare yesterday, where a 2-year-old was resisting a rest.

If artists wear sketchers do linguists wear converse?

I changed my iPod name to Titanic. It's syncing now.

Jill broke her finger today, but on the other hand she was completely fine.

I smeared some ketchup all over my eyes once. It was a bad idea in Heinz- sight.

I flipped a coin over an issue the other day, it was quite the toss-up.

I got hit in the head with a can of soda? Luckily it was a soft drink.

I heard that the post office was a male dominated industry.

Why isn't suntanning an Olympic sport? Because the best you can ever get is bronze.

Why is Kylo Ren so angry? Beause he's always Ben Solo.

These reversing cameras are great. Since I got one I haven't looked back.

The candle quit his job because he felt burned out.

Our maintenance guy lost his legs on the job, now he's just a handyman.

A magic tractor drove down the road and turned into a field!

I met some aliens from outer space. They were pretty down to earth.

The plane flight brought my acrophobia to new heights.

My phone has to wear glasses ever since it lost its contacts.

The show was called Spongebob Squarepants but everyone knows the star was Patrick.

Novice pirates make terrible singers because they can't hit the high seas.

I told my friend she drew her eyebrows too high. She seemed surprised.

If I buy a bigger bed will I have more or less bedroom?

Two peanuts were walking in a tough neighborhood and one of them was a-salted.

Two ropes were walking in a tough neighborhood and one of them was a-frayed.

I got a master's degree in being ignored; no one seems to care.

After eating the ship, the sea monster said, I can't believe I ate the hull thing.

Smaller babies may be delivered by stork but the heavier ones need a crane.

A bartender broke up with her boyfriend, but he kept asking her for another shot.

He couldn't work out how to fix the washing machine so he threw in the towel.

Why does the man want to buy nine rackets? Cause tennis too many.

Why don't cannibals eat clowns? Because they taste funny.

If I got paid in lots of Pennes I would make loads of pasta.

I thought I saw a spider on my laptop, but my friend said it was just a bug.

A doctor broke his leg while auditioning for a play.Luckily he still made the cast.

The tale of the haunted refrigerator was chilling.

Why are frogs so happy? They eat whatever bugs them.

If you wear cowboy clothes are you ranch dressing?

I was addicted to the hokey pokey but I turned myself around.

Simba, you're falling behind. I must ask you to Mufasa.

I feel sorry for shopping carts. They're always getting pushed around.

The display of still-life art was not at all moving!

Why couldn't the dead car drive into the cluttered garage? Lack of vroom.

What do you call Samsung's security guards? Guardians of the Galaxy.

How does a penguin build it's house? Igloos it together.

Time flies like an arrow. Fruit flies like a banana.

The safe was invented by a cop and a robber. It was quite a combination.

What do you do when balloons are hurt? You helium.

One hat says to the other, "You stay here, I'll go on a head."

-----

4

301 - 400

When the scientist wanted to clone a deer, he bought a doe it yourself kit.

If people ask how many puns I made in Germany I reply, "nein"

Did you hear about the invention of the white board? It was remarkable.

If Donald Trump becomes president, America is going toupee.

I hate Russian Dolls, they are so full of themselves.

The magazine about ceiling fans went out of business due to low circulation.

So what if I don't know what apocalypse means? It's not the end of the world!

Some aquatic mammals at the zoo escaped. It was otter chaos.

I asked my friend, Nick, if he had 5 cents I could borrow. But he was Nicholas.

There's a fine line between the numerator and the denominator.

I used to work at a hairdresser but i just wasn't cut out for it.

Why is metal and a microwave a match made in heaven? When they met, sparks flew.

The lumberjack loved his new computer. He especially enjoyed logging in.

When the church relocated it had an organ transplant.

Lettuce take a moment to appreciate this salad pun.

The scarecrow get promoted because he was outstanding in his field.

Sleeping comes so naturally to me, I could do it with my eyes closed.

I never understood odorless chemicals, they never make scents.

What do prisoners use to call each other? Cell phones.

When a clock is hungry, it goes back four seconds.

Did you hear about the pun that was actually funny? Neither have we.

Want to hear a pun about ghosts? That's the spirit!

I used to make clown shoes... which was no small feat.

Did you hear about the human cannonball? Too bad he got fired!

What happened when the magician got mad? She pulled her hare out!

Did you hear about the circus that caught on fire? It was in tents.

The one day of the week that eggs are definitely afraid of is Fry-day.

A hen will always leave her house through the proper eggs-it.

The man who ate too many eggs was considered to be an egg-oholic.

All the hens consider the chef to be very mean because he beats the eggs.

Eskimos keep all of their chilled eggs inside of the egg-loo.

Under the doctor's advice, the hen is laying off eggs for a few weeks.

I had a real problem making a hard-boiled egg this morning until I cracked it.

The best time of day to eat eggs is at the crack of dawn.

The chicken coop only had 2 doors since if it had 4 doors it would be a sedan.

Crossing a cement mixer and a chicken will result in you getting a brick layer.

That reckless little egg always seems to egg-celerate when he sees the light turn yellow.

Hopefully this egg pun doesn't make your brain too fried or scrambled.

Don't ever have multiple people wash dishes together. It's hard for them to stay in sink.

People using umbrellas always seem to be under the weather.

I dissected an iris today. It was an eye-opening experience.

What was Forrest Gump's email password? 1forrest1.

What planet is like a circus? Saturn, it has three rings!

Before my father died he worked in a circus as a stilt walker. I used to look up to him.

Why did the lion eat the tightrope walker? He wanted a well-balanced meal!

I hate negative numbers and will stop at nothing to avoid them.

Did you hear about the restaurant on the moon? Great food, no atmosphere.

Want to hear a joke about paper? Nevermind it's tearable.

I just watched a program about beavers. It was the best dam program I've ever seen.

Why did the coffee file a police report? It got mugged.

How does a penguin build it's house? Igloos it together.

Dad, did you get a haircut? No I got them all cut.

What do you call a Mexican who has lost his car? Carlos.

Dad, can you put my shoes on? No, I don't think they'll fit me.

Why did the scarecrow win an award? Because he was outstanding in his field.

Why don't skeletons ever go trick or treating? Because they have no body to go with.

Ill call you later. Don't call me later, call me Dad.

What do you call an elephant that doesn't matter? An irrelephant

-----

Want to hear a joke about construction? I'm still working on it.

What do you call cheese that isn't yours? Nacho Cheese.

What did the grape do when he got stepped on? He let out a little wine.

Dad, can you put the cat out? I didn't know it was on fire.

This graveyard looks overcrowded. People must be dying to get in there.

5/4 of people admit that they're bad with fractions.

Two goldfish are in a tank. One says to the other, "do you know how to drive this thing?"

What do you call a man with a rubber toe? Roberto.

What do you call a fat psychic? A four-chin teller.

I would avoid the sushi if I was you. It's a little fishy.

To the man in the wheelchair that stole my camouflage jacket... You can hide but you can't run.

I thought about going on an all-almond diet. But that's just nuts

-----

I've never gone to a gun range before. I decided to give it a shot!

Why do you never see elephants hiding in trees? Because they're so good at it.

Did you hear about the kidnapping at school? It's fine, he woke up.

A furniture store keeps calling me. All I wanted was one night stand.

I used to work in a shoe recycling shop. It was sole destroying.

Did I tell you the time I fell in love during a backflip? I was heels over head.

I don't play soccer because I enjoy the sport. I'm just doing it for kicks.

People don't like having to bend over to get their drinks. We really need to raise the bar.

Today at the bank, an old lady asked me to help check her balance. So I pushed her over.

I told my girlfriend she drew her eyebrows too high. She seemed surprised.

My dog used to chase people on a bike a lot. It got so bad, finally I had to take his bike away.

I'm so good at sleeping. I can do it with my eyes closed.

My boss told me to have a good day.. so I went home.

Why do blind people hate skydiving? It scares the hell out of their dogs.

When you look really closely, all mirrors look like eyeballs.

My friend says to me: "What rhymes with orange" I

said: "No it doesn't"

What do you call a guy with a rubber toe? Roberto.

What did the pirate say when he turned 80 years old? Aye matey.

My wife told me I had to stop acting like a flamingo. So I had to put my foot down.

I couldn't figure out why the baseball kept getting larger. Then it hit me.

Why did the old man fall in the well? Because he couldn't see that well.

I ate a clock yesterday, it was very time consuming.

Whatdya call a frenchman wearing sandals? Phillipe Phillope.

A blind man walks into a bar. And a table. And a chair.

I know a lot of jokes about unemployed people but none of them work.

Did you hear about the italian chef that died? He pasta way.

Why couldn't the bicycle stand up? Because it was two tired!

Parallel lines have so much in common. It's a shame they'll never meet.

My wife accused me of being immature. I told her to get out of my fort.

Where do you find a cow with no legs? Right where you left it.

-----

5

401 - 500

When a deaf person sees someone yawn do they think it's a scream?

As I suspected, someone has been adding soil to my garden. The plot thickens.

How do crazy people go through the forest? They take the physco path.

What did the traffic light say to the car? Don't look! I'm about to change.

I just wrote a book on reverse psychology. Do *not* read it!

What did one hat say to the other? You stay here. I'll go on ahead.

Why wouldn't the shrimp share his treasure? Because he was a little shellfish.

If laughter is the best medicine, your face must be curing the world.

You're so ugly, you scared the crap out of the toilet.

Your family tree must be a cactus because everybody on it is a prick.

It's better to let someone think you are an Idiot than to open your mouth and prove it.

Your birth certificate is an apology letter from the condom factory.

I guess you prove that even god makes mistakes sometimes.

The only way you'll ever get laid is if you crawl up a chicken's ass and wait.

You're so ugly, when your mom dropped you off at school she got a fine for littering.

If I wanted to kill myself I'd climb your ego and jump to your IQ.

You must have been born on a highway because that's where most accidents happen.

Brains aren't everything. In your case they're nothing.

I don't know what makes you so stupid, but it really works.

I can explain it to you, but I can't understand it for you.

Roses are red violets are blue, God made me pretty, what happened to you?

Behind every fat woman there is a beautiful woman. No seriously, your in the way.

Calling you an idiot would be an insult to all the stupid people.

Some babies were dropped on their heads but you were clearly thrown at a wall.

Don't like my sarcasm, well I don't like your stupid.

They say opposites attract. I hope you meet someone who is good-looking, intelligent, and cultured.

Stop trying to be a smart ass, you're just an ass.

The last time I saw something like you, I flushed it.

You have Diarrhea of the mouth; constipation of the ideas.

Your mind is on vacation but your mouth is working overtime.

Why don't you slip into something more comfortable... like a coma.

If your gonna be two faced, honey at least make one of them pretty.

Keep rolling your eyes, perhaps you'll find a brain
back there.

You are not as bad as people say, you are much,
much worse.

I don't know what your problem is, but I'll bet it's
hard to pronounce.

You get ten times more girls than me? ten times zero
is zero...

You're the reason the gene pool needs a lifeguard.

Sure, I've seen people like you before - but I had to
pay an admission.

How old are you? - Wait I shouldn't ask, you can't
count that high.

Have you been shopping lately? They're selling lives,
you should go get one.

Of course I talk like an idiot, how else would you
understand me?

To make you laugh on Saturday, I need to you joke on Wednesday.

I'd like to see things from your point of view but I can't seem to get my head that far up my ass.

Your house is so dirty you have to wipe your feet before you go outside.

If you really spoke your mind, you'd be speechless.

You are so old, when you were a kid rainbows were black and white.

If I told you that I have a piece of dirt in my eye, would you move?

You so dumb, you think Cheerios are doughnut seeds.

So, a thought crossed your mind? Must have been a long and lonely journey.

Every time I'm next to you, I get a fierce desire to be alone.

Keep talking, someday you'll say something
intelligent!

How did you get here? Did someone leave your cage
open?

Pardon me, but you've obviously mistaken me for
someone who gives a damn.

Wipe your mouth, there's still a tiny bit of bullshit
around your lips.

Don't you have a terribly empty feeling - in your
skull?

As an outsider, what do you think of the human
race?

Just because you have one doesn't mean you have to
act like one.

We can always tell when you are lying. Your lips
move.

Are you always this stupid or is today a special
occasion?

What do you call a cow that just had a baby? DeCALFeinated or A New Moother

-----

What kind of fish is made of only 2 sodium atoms? 2 Na

I don't trust stairs. They're always up to something.

If you want a job in the moisturizer industry, the best advice I can give is to apply daily.

When my wife told me to stop impersonating a flamingo, I had to put my foot down.

What do you call a can of soup that eats other cans of soup? A CANnibal.

Why can't you hear a pterodactyl using the bathroom? Because the P is silent.

Want to hear a joke about construction? Nah, I'm still working on it.

You heard the rumor going around about butter? Nevermind, I shouldn't spread it.

What concert costs only 45 cents? 50 Cent ft. Nickelback

Son: Where are my sunglasses? Dad: I don't know...where are my dad glasses?

What do they call Miley Cyrus in Europe? Kilometry Cyprus.

I have kleptomania. Sometimes when it gets really bad, I take something for it.

You shouldn't kiss anyone on January 1st because it's only the first date.

If a child refuses to take a nap, is he resisting a rest?

Want to hear my pizza joke? Never mind, it's too cheesy.

A furniture store keeps calling me. But all I wanted was one night stand.

Why does Peter pan always fly? Because he neverlands!

My wife told me I was average, I think she's mean.

I gave all my dead batteries away today... Free of charge.

Just quit my job at Starbucks because day after day it was the same old grind.

Went to the corner shop today... Bought four corners.

I'm thinking about getting a new haircut... I'm going to mullet over.

I wouldn't buy anything with velcro. It's a total rip-off.

Why couldn't the bicycle stand up by itself? It was two tired.

What do you call Santa's helpers? Subordinate clauses.

I used to have a job at the calendar factory, but they fired me because I took a couple of days off.

You got a haircut? Looks like you got all of them cut!

I owe a lot to the sidewalks. They've been keeping me off the streets for years.

Atoms are untrustworthy little critters. They make up everything!

What do you call a man in a pond who has no legs and no arms? - Bob.

I spent days making a wooden car with wooden wheels. It just wooden work.

Thank you, my arms, for always being there by my side.

Have you heard about the Italian cook with an incurable disease? He pastaway.

What do you receive when you ask a lemon for help? Lemonaid.

What does a dog say when he sits down on a piece of sandpaper? Ruff!

A man sued an airline company after it lost his luggage. Sadly, he lost his case.

What is a typical diet of a sea monster? Fish and ships.

Shouldn't pregnant women be called body builders?

What would you call an obese psychic? - A four-chin teller.

If goods get damaged in transport, does it become 'bads'?

-----

6

501 - 600

What do you call the wife of a hippie? A Mississippi.

What should a proper lawyer wear to a court? - A good law suit.

When does a car stop being a car? - The second it turns into a driveway.

Somebody stole all my lamps. I couldn't be more delighted.

What happens when you cross a snowman and a vampire? - A: You get a frostbite.

The local gene pool looks like it could use quite a bit of chlorine.

What should you call an absolutely average potato? A commentator.

Have you heard about the fire in the shoe factory? Hundreds of soles were lost!

What do you get if you crossbreed a cute Easter rabbit with an insect? Bugs Bunny.

Why are Apple staff absolutely forbidden to fart in Apple stores? Because there are no windows.

Why does your dog run into the corner each time the bell rings? - He's a Boxer.

I just stepped on some Cheerios on the floor. - You can call me a cereal killer now!

Why did the calf cross the road? It wanted to get to the udder side.

Once you contract an infection of the bladder, urine trouble.

How do you make a good egg-roll? You push it down a hill.

Q: How do you make a tissue dance? - A: Just needs a little boogey!

What kind of a driver doesn't know how to drive? The screwdriver.

Salt meets pepper on a plate and says, "I'm feeling all scattered today."

I was recently diagnosed with color-blindness. It came out of the green.

Q: Why did the lights go out? A: They liked each other a lot.

Who said grapes are soft? They never cry when you step on them, they just let out a bit of wine.

What did I do when I landed in Iraq by mistake? - Iran.

I heard Apple is designing a new automatic car. But

they're having trouble installing windows.

Stairs cannot be trusted. They're always UP to something.

I nearly drowned yesterday. It was a breathtaking experience.

This may come across as cheesy - but I think you're grate.

What does a cloud with an itchy rash do? - Finds the nearest skyscraper.

The future, the present, and the past walk into a shady bar.Things get tense.

What would you call a female magician in the desert? - A sandwich.

Why did the banana have to go to the doctor? It wasn't peeling too well.

Sure, I drink brake fluid. But I can stop anytime, no problem!

I've started sleeping in our fireplace. Now I sleep like a log!

The most exciting beverage for a soccer player? The penaltea!

I once worked in a bank, but then I lost interest.

Why was Cinderella kicked off the soccer team? She always ran away from the ball.

What do you get when you crossbreed fish with elephants? Swimming trunks.

Oh you are gluten free? So you go against the grain? Pasta la vista baby.

How to achieve a beach body? 1. Have a body 2. Arrive at the beach.

Getting fat wasn't my intention. It was a pure and clear snaccident.

What did the fish say when it hit its head on a wall? Dam!!!

Coffee is the silent victim in our house. It gets mugged every day.

A group of termites marches into a saloon and ask: "Is the bar tender here?"

I wonder why there aren't any more cemeteries around. People are really dying to get in there.

What were the words of a truck driver after he got a flat? Darn, this is a wheely bad time.

I cannot stand insect puns. They bug the heck out of me.

Two egotists started a fight. It was an I for an I.

A man in a butcher shop: "I would like bull testicles please." - Butcher: "Me too."

I was trying to catch some fog earlier but I mist.

Why did the octopus blush? He'd just seen the bottom of the ocean.

Why does Peter Pan fly all the time? - He

Neverlands.

Why are programmers no fans of the outdoors? - There are too many bugs.

I'd love to know how the Earth rotates. It would totally make my day.

Why is the math book so sad? - It's got too many problems.

How do you organize a fantastic space party? You planet.

Why was the tomato all red? It saw the salad dressing.

What would you call a fish with a missing eye? A fsh, probably.

I wanted to tell you a joke about leeches. But I won't – they all suck.

What lies on the ocean bed and is twitching uncontrollably? A nervous wreck.

I've seen this show about beavers last night – best dam documentary I've ever seen!"

Why do mathematicians tend to marry larger women? - Because they like curves.

What do you call somebody who keeps abandoning their diet plans? - A desserter.

You're becoming a vegetarian? I think that's a big missed steak.

Where do cows like to go in their spare time? In the Muuuuuuseum.

Do you know how they make holy water? They boil the hell out of it!

Were French fries originally made in France? - Nope, French fries have always been made in Greece!

I know that I'm fat but I'd be really rich in Britain. There they measure their wealth in pounds.

Two wi-fi antennas got married last Saturday. The reception was fantastic.

It's not nice making fun of fat people. They've got enough on their plates as it is.

What is red and occasionally explodes in the fruit section? - A pomegranate.

If a wild pig kills you, does it mean you've been boared to death?

What was the football coach yelling at the vending machine? "Gimme my quarter back!!!"

What do snowmen do in their spare time? - Just chilling.

Jokes about unemployed people are not funny. They just don't work.

What to say to a hitch-hiker with just one leg? Hop in.

"Why is there music coming out of your printer?" - "That will be the paper jamming again!"

What do you get when you cross a bear with a skunk? Winnie the Pooh.

How to catch a squirrel? - Go in a forest and act nuts.

My ex-wife still misses me. But her aim is steadily improving.

My socks got really holy. I can only wear them to church.

Whenever I undress in the bathroom, my shower gets turned on.

If you spent your day in a well, can you say your day was well-spent?

A guy was admitted to hospital with 8 plastic horses in his stomach. His condition is now stable.

Why did the balloon go near the needle? He wanted to be a pop star.

I was hoping to steal some leftovers from the party but I guess my plans were foiled.

I got very lonely lately, so I bought some shares. It's much nicer having some company.

Which country's capital is the fastest growing? Ireland's. Every year it's Dublin.

Why was the chef arrested? - He was beating eggs every day.

Never date cross eyed people. They might be seeing somebody on the side!

Apparently taking a day off is not something you should do when you work for a calendar company.

What did the Buddhist ask the hot dog vendor? "Make me one with everything."

You know why you never see elephants hiding up in trees? Because they're really good at it.

What is red and smells like blue paint? Red paint.

Where does the General keep his armies? In his sleevies!

Why aren't koalas actual bears? The don't meet the koalafications.

Why don't blind people skydive? Because it scares the crap out of their dogs.

I saw a wino eating grapes. I told him, you gotta wait. (Mitch Hedberg)

What does a pepper do when it's angry? It gets jalapeño face!

Two gold fish are in a tank. One looks at the other and says, "You know how to drive this thing?!"

Two soldiers are in a tank. One looks at the other and says, "BLUBLUBBLUBLUBBLUB."

As a scarecrow, people say I'm outstanding in my field. But hay, it's in my jeans.

-----

7

601 - 700

How did the hipster burn his mouth? He ate the pizza before it was cool.

What's the difference between an oral thermometer and a rectal thermometer? The taste.

An atheist, a Crossfitter, and a vegan walk into a bar. I know because they told me.

I waited and stayed up all night and tried to figure out where the sun was. Then it dawned on me.

I told my friend 10 jokes to get him to laugh. Sadly, no pun in 10 did.

What's red and moves up and down? A tomato in an elevator

I bought the world's worst thesaurus yesterday. Not only is it terrible, it's terrible.

Why can't you hear a pterodactyl go to the bathroom? Because the "P" is silent!

How did the blonde die ice fishing? She was hit by the zamboni.

How Long is a Chinese man's name. No, it actually is.

What's a pirates favorite letter? You think it's R but it be the C.

Have you heard about corduroy pillows? They're making headlines.

What did the green grape say to the purple grape? OMG!!!!!!! BREATHE!! BREATHEEEEE!!!!!

What do Alexander the Great and Winnie the Pooh have in common? Same middle name.

My grandfather died peacefully, in his sleep......not screaming like the passengers in his car.

What did the left eye say to the right eye? Between you and me, something smells.

What do Cannon Balls do when they're in love? Make bbs.

Why did the cowboy get a wiener dog? He wanted to get a long little doggie.

Sometimes I tuck my knees into my chest and lean forward. That's just how I roll.

I intend to live forever. So far, so good. (Steve Wright)

Thanks for explaining the word "many" to me, it means a lot.

Most people are shocked when they find out how bad I am as an electrician

-----

Why did the cross-eyed teacher lose her job?

Because she couldn't control her pupils.

To the mathematicians who thought of the idea of zero, thanks for nothing!

I just found out I'm colorblind. The diagnosis came completely out of the purple.

Just burned 2,000 calories. That's the last time I leave brownies in the oven while I nap.

The future, the present and the past walked into a bar. Things got a little tense.

-----

eBay is so useless. I tried to look up lighters and all they had was 13,749 matches.

I saw an ad for burial plots, and thought to myself this is the last thing I need.

Claustrophobic people are more productive thinking out of the box.

I was addicted to the hokey pokey... but thankfully, I turned myself around.

What do you call a dictionary on drugs? HIGH-Definition.

Atheists don't solve exponential equations because they don't believe in higher powers.

A mexican magician was doing a magic trick. He said, Uno, Dose, and he disappeared without a trace

-----

What is the best thing about living in Switzerland? Well, the flag is a big plus.

What did E.T.'s mother say to him when he got home? "Where on Earth have you been?!"

My wife likes it when I blow air on her when she's hot, but honestly... I'm not a fan.

What do you call a priest that becomes a lawyer? A father in law.

I accidentally handed my wife a glue stick instead of a chapstick. She still isn't talking to me.

Q: What do you call the security outside of a Samsung Store? A: Guardians of the Galaxy.

If a short psychic broke out of jail, then you'd have a small medium at large.

I ordered 2000 lbs. of chinese soup. It was Won Ton.

Why couldn't the leopard play hide and seek? Because he was always spotted.

Got my girlfriend a "get better soon" card. She's not sick, I just think she could get better.

Oxygen is proven to be a toxic gas. Anyone who inhales oxygen will normally dies within 80 years.

I can't believe I got fired from the calendar factory. All I did was take a day off.

I'm reading a book about anti-gravity. It's impossible to put down.

A termite walks into a bar and says, "Where is the bar tender?"

I wasn't originally going to get a brain transplant, but then I changed my mind.

A courtroom artist was arrested today for an unknown reason... details are sketchy.

Dr.'s are saying not to worry about the bird flu because it's tweetable.

I've decided to sell my Hoover... well, it was just collecting dust.

For Halloween we dressed up as almonds. Everyone could tell we were nuts.

My boss says I intimidate the other employees, so I just stared at him until he apologized.

Police have arrested the World tongue-twister Champion. I imagine he'll be given a tough sentence.

Heard about the drug addict fisherman who accidentally caught a duck? Now he's hooked on the quack.

Why was Cinderella thrown off the basketball team? She ran away from the ball.

I've just written a song about tortillas - actually, it's more of a rap.

I'd tell you a chemistry joke but I know I wouldn't get a reaction.

If 4 out of 5 people SUFFER from diarrhea... does that mean that one enjoys it?

I had a neck brace fitted years ago and I've never looked back since.

Why do seagulls fly over the sea? Because if they flew over the bay they'd be bagels!

If a child refuses to sleep during nap time, are they guilty of resisting a rest?

What do you call a laughing motorcycle? A Yamahahaha.

I have a few jokes about unemployed people but it doesn't matter none of them work.

Why do the French eat snails? They don't like fast food.

I found a rock yesterday which measured 1760 yards in length. Must be some kind of milestone.

My boss is going to fire the employee with the worst posture. I have a hunch, it might be me.

My doctors office has two doctors on call at all times. Is that considered a pair a docs.

What did one eye say to the other eye? Between you and me something smells.

My boss told me to have a good day. So I went home.

This morning some clown opened the door for me. I thought to myself that's a nice Jester.

Did you hear about these new reversible jackets? I'm excited to see how they turn out.

Did you hear about the man who jumped off a bridge in France? He was in Sein.

The first time I got a universal remote control, I thought to myself "This changes everything".

Justice is a dish best served cold because if it were served warm, it would be justwater.

Cleaning mirrors is a job I could really see myself doing.

I'm emotionally constipated. I haven't given a shit in days.

Why don't aliens visit our planet? Terrible ratings. One star.

Why did the picture end up in jail? It was framed!

Did you hear about the 2 silk worms in a race? It ended in a tie!

I was born to be a pessimist. My blood type is B Negative.

How did Jesus' crucifixion save us? It's 'cause he nailed it!

What do you call a cow during an earthquake? A milkshake.

My first job was working in an orange juice factory, but I got canned: couldn't concentrate.

When I get naked in the bathroom, the shower usually gets turned on.

Three conspiracy theorists walk into a bar. You can't tell me that's just a coincidence!

I'm reading a horror story in Braille. Something bad is about to happen... I can feel it.

Just had a date with a woman who welds for a living and oh my, were the sparks flying.

Why did the scientist install a knocker on his door? He wanted to win the No-bell prize!

A book just fell on my head. I've only got myshelf to blame.

Why couldn't the bike stand up on it's own? It was two tired.

Did you hear about the depressed plumber? He's been going through some shit.

Someone broke into my house last night and stole my Limbo stick. How low can you get?

What do you have to do to have a party in space? You have to Planet.

I always wanted to learn to procrastinate... just never got around to it.

I am on a seafood diet. Every time I see food, I eat it.

Q: What do you call a cow with a twitch? A: "Beef Jerky!"

I'm no photographer, but I can picture us together.

What was Forrest Gump's email password? "1forrest1"

8

I had a job tying sausages together, but I couldn't make ends meet.

Last time I got caught stealing a calendar I got 12 months.

I got a part in a movie called "Cocaine". I only have one line.

My computer's got Miley Virus. It has stopped twerking.

I tried to escape the Apple store. I couldn't because there were no Windows.

As a wizard, I enjoy turning objects into a glass. Just wanted to make that clear.

I relish the fact that you've mustard the strength to ketchup to me.

Why was the horse so happy? Because he lived in a stable environment.

I couldn't quite remember how to throw a boomerang, but eventually, it came back to me.

I used to wonder why Frisbees looked bigger the closer it came... Then it hit me!

I threw an Asian man down a flight of stairs. It was Wong on so many levels.

Did you hear about the Italian chef with a terminal illness? He pastaway.

Me: "You said dress for the job you want." Boss: "Give me my clothes back."

People don't get my puns. They think they're funny.

Why was the tree excited about the future? It was ready to turn over a new leaf!

When I was young, I always felt like a male trapped in a females body. Then I was born

-----

Why did the bee get married? Because he found his honey.

Someone stole my toilet and the police have nothing to go on.

To the guy who invented the number zero: "Thanks for nothing".

Having sex in an elevator is wrong on so many levels.

I'm trying to date a philosophy professor, but she doesn't even know if I exist or not.

What's the best place to grow flowers in school?... In the kindergarden.

What do you call people who are afraid of Santa Claus? Claustrophobic

-----

I just found an origami porn channel, but it is paper view only.

What is the name of an Asian pilot who died in a plane crash? Sum Ting Wong.

The doctor told his patient to stop using a Q-tip, but it went in one ear and out the other.

Anyone who wanted to sell fish had to get permission from grandpa. He was known as the cod father.

I used to work at a fire hydrant factory couldn't park nowhere near the place.

What do you call a girl standing in the middle of a tennis court? Annette.

How can you spot the blind guy at the nudist colony? It's not hard.

What happens if you eat yeast and shoe polish? Every morning you will rise and shine!

It's hard to explain puns to kleptomaniacs because they always take things literally.

Hung a picture up on the wall the other day. Nailed it.

Why don't you ever see hippos hiding in trees? Because they are really good at it.

Tried watching The Neverending Story, couldn't finish it.

I was going to give him a nasty look, but he already had one.

What do you call a horse who expresses negative views? A Naysayer.

A hole was found in the wall of a nudist camp. The police are looking into it.

My IQ test results just came in and I'm really relieved. Thank God it's negative.

What is the best Christmas present ever? A broken drum - you can't beat it!

What do sea monsters eat for lunch? Fish and ships.

What do you get when you cross a snoman and a vampire? Frost bite.

Sang the rainbow song in front of a police officer, got arrested for colourful language

-----

Isn't it scary that doctors call what they do "practice"?

Why did the scarecrow win the competition? He was 'outstanding' in his field!

I threw a boomerang many years ago. I now live in constant fear.

What do you call an academically successful slice of bread? An honor roll.

Two windmills are standing in a field and one asks the other, "What kind of music do you like?"

No matter how much you push the envelope, it'll still be stationery.

I know I know, smoking's bad for me and all. But, my mama told me never to be a quitter.

What concert costs 45 cents? 50 Cent feat. Nickelback.

My tennis opponent was not happy with my serve. He kept returning it.

For Sale: Parachute. Only used once, never opened.

Why do Swedish warships have barcodes on them? So when they dock they can Scandinavian.

A garage sale is actually a Garbage sale but the "b" is silent.

What do you call Watson when Sherlock isn't around? Holmeless.

I'm taking part in a stair climbing competition. Guess I better step up my game.

Did you hear about the vegan transgender? He was a herbefore.

Went to quite a few stores to find the best prices for herbs... I think it was thyme well spent.

If anything is possible, is it possible for something to be impossible?

Heard about the pilot who decided to cook whilst flying? It was a recipe for disaster.

People often ask me if my French jokes are immature... wee.

Why doesn't the bike stand by itself? Because it's two tired.

How do you make a fire with two sticks? Make sure one of them is a match!

Why was Cinderella banned from playing sports? Because she always ran away from the ball.

There's safety in Numbers, but I prefer Deuteronomy.

What musical instrument is found in the bathroom?
A tuba toothpaste.

Q: What happens to the man who lost his whole left side of his body?

Where does the Easter Bunny go to eat pancakes? To IHOP, of course!

What happened when the semicolon broke grammar laws? It was given two consecutive sentences.

If the koreans cannot do it, they will tell you that they won do it.

Why don't oysters share their pearls? Because they're shellfish.

I'm very pleased with my new fridge magnet. So far I've got twelve fridges.

I put a new freezer next to the refrigerator, now they're just chilling.

At my job, I have 500 people under me. I'm a security guard at a cemetery.

What's the difference between a Harley and a vacuum cleaner? The position of the dirtbag.

You can't get on the same page with someone who has a different book.

My new girlfriend works at the Zoo. I think she is a keeper.

My Sister was crying so I asked her if she was having a cry-sis.

How does a snowman get around? He rides an icicle!

I used to build stairs for a living, it's an up and down business.

Maybe it's not global warming. Maybe it's just planetary menopause.

I once worked as a salesman and was very independent; I took orders from no one.

Why did the M&M go to school? Because he really wanted to be a Smartie!

I got a job in a health club, but they said I wasn't fit for the job.

They say "don't try this at home" so I'm coming over to your house to try it...

I Googled "how to start a wildfire". I got 48,500 matches.

The video from the ring infects people with airborne pathogens. The video went viral.

I told my girlfriend she drew her eyebrows too high. She seemed looked.

What do you call a Russian procrastinator? Putinoff.

Whats long and hard and has cum in it? A cucumber.

Golfer: "I'd move heaven and earth to break 100 on this course."

Caddy: "Try heaven; you've already moved most of the earth."

What do you get when you cross a joke with a rhetorical question?

Why do people become butchers? So they can meat people.

I would make jokes about the sea, but they are too deep.

What do you call it when two transgender midgets have sex? Micro trans-action.

Why do women have cleaner minds than men? Because they change theirs more often.

Television is a medium because anything well done is rare.

I find it very offensive when people get easily offended.

-----

9

801 - 900

Teacher: "Where was the Constitution of India signed?"

I remember being in so much debt that I couldn't afford my electricity bills, it was a dark time.

How did the soggy Easter Bunny dry himself? With a hare dryer!

Iron Man is a very confusing character. I know he's a guy but he could have been Fe Male.

Why shouldn't you make fun of a paleontologist? Because you will get Jurasskicked.

Two cheese trucks ran into each other. De brie was everywhere.

What did the blanket say when it fell off the bed? "Oh sheet!"

How many tickles does it take to make an octopus laugh? Ten tickles.

Why did the Investigator question the flat iron? To straighten things out.

How did the chemist who failed the temperature test get? Absolute zero.

What do you call your sister if she only has one leg? Eileen.

Don't listen to Google. You are a strong, confident password.

Will glass coffins be a success? Remains to be seen.

I wonder why there are locks on the doors of Seven-Eleven when it says they are open 24/7.

Why was there thunder and lightning in the lab? The scientists were brainstorming!

Scientist: "My findings are meaningless if taken out of context."

Media: Scientist claims "Findings are meaningless."

Why was it so hot in the stadium after the baseball game? All the fans left!

Why did the duck get arrested? Because he was selling quack.

Do you know why I make puns? Because it's my respunsibility.

What did the vegan say? I made a big missed steak.

Just got a job as senior director at Old McDonald's Farm. I'm the CIEIO.

I just got this sick job at the Calendar factory. Unfortunately, I still can't get a date.

I figure I might need a new kidney in 30 years, so I've decided to have a kid.

Why did the lion broke up with his girlfriend? Because she was a cheetah!

Why do soccer players do so well in math? They know how to use their heads!

I made a graph of my past relationships. It has an ex axis and a why axis.

Why are fish never good tennis players? They don't like getting close to the net.

The person who invented the door knock won the No-bell prize.

Why did St. Patrick drive all the snakes out of Ireland? He couldn't afford plane fare.

Why can't fishermen be generous? Because their business makes them sell fish!

Did you hear about the pessimist who hates German sausage? He always fears the Wurst.

What did the little mountain say to the big mountain? Hi Cliff!

I once dated a woman who uses a nightlight. What a turn off.

What does a mathematician say when something goes wrong? Figures!

One day we shall wake up together: me and my money.

I used to be a boy trapped in a woman's body. But after 9 long months, I was finally born!

Just gonna have a quick nap because I heard you can sleep your way to the top.

Give a man a gun and he will rob a bank. Give a man a bank and he will rob everyone.

Why should you wary of stairs? Because they are always up to something.

Do skunks celebrate Valentine's Day? Sure, they're

very scent-imental!

Love is like a machine... sometimes you need a good screw to fix it.

Where did the spaghetti and the sauce go dancing? The meatball!

What do you call someone who is afraid of picnics? A basket case!

My midget friend got thrown out of the nudist colony because he kept getting in everyone's hair.

Today I have met the vegetarian brother of Bruce Lee. Brocco Lee.

What was the barristas favourite part about being arrested? The mug shots.

I lost my paper towels, I think I need a bounty hunter.

I worked in the woods as a lumberjack, but I just couldn't hack it, so they gave me the ax.

What did the paper say to the pencil? You've got a good point!

Why did the broom get a poor grade in school? Because it was always sweeping during class!

What did the doctor say to the alcoholic? Keep taking the Pils.

Why are spiders great tennis players? Cause they have great topspin.

Did you hear about the hungry clock? It went back four seconds!

I screamed at my neighbor, "What on earth are you doing on our roof!"

He screamed back, "I saw you at the bar, and you said the drinks were on the house!"

Why did the octopus beat the shark in a fight? Because the octopus was well armed.

Pork and Leek... great flavor for sausages... lousy brand name for condoms.

Why is a doctor always calm? Because it has a lot of patients.

Where do frogs deposit their money? In a river bank.

Nothing is impossible. The word itself says "I'm possible."

What do you call the trousers of people who can't speak? Pant-O-Mimes!

When is a field hockey player like a judge? When she sits on the bench.

Shocked by the Sears news today, I had no idea it was still open.

What do you call a fake noodle? An Impasta.

Whenever the cashier at the grocery store asks my dad if he would like the milk in a bag he replies, "No, just leave it in the carton!"

A woman walks into a library and asked if they had

any books about paranoia. The librarian says "They're right behind you!"

The other day, my wife asked me to pass her lipstick but I accidentally passed her a glue stick. She still isn't talking to me.

And the lord said unto John, "Come forth and you will receive eternal life". John came fifth and won a toaster.

My psychiatrist told me I was crazy and I said I want a second opinion. He said okay, you're ugly too.

My friend thinks he is smart. He told me an onion is the only food that makes you cry, so I threw a coconut at his face.

So I came home from work yesterday to find that someone broke into my apartment. Looking around, it seemed like they didn't really take a whole lot. My TV was still there, my PS4, and my legos were fine. But the apartment was dark, even when I tried to turn on the lights. Seems the only thing that was taken were my lightbulbs and a couple lamps...I was delighted.

What's the difference between a hippo and a zippo? One is really heavy and the other is a little lighter.

My wife is on a tropical food diet, the house is full of the stuff. It's enough to make a mango crazy.

Imagine if you would hit the clock in the morning and the clock would hit you right back. - I think it would be truly alarming.

A woman was just taking a bath when she heard the doorbell. She thought she'd just pretend not to be home but then the ringer called, "Hello? Anybody home? I'm the blind guy!" "Ah well, if he is blind I can go and open the door just like this. No need to dress." thought the lady, hauled herself out of the bath and went to open the door. "Wow," said the guy waiting there, "you should be on a fitness studio advertisement! Now, where should I put those blinds?"

What did the mayonnaise say when somebody opened the refrigerator door? - Close the door, will you? I'm dressing!

Aim for the stars! But first take care of the bodyguards. Why is a skeleton a bad liar? - You can see right through it.

How to spot a blind man on a nudist beach? Well it's not hard, really... Where should a dog go when it's lost its tail? The retail store of course.

One skeleton to the other: Man, I'm so hard in love with Bella, I can barely think straight. I'd love to ask her out but I just don't have the guts.

-----

37 consonants, 25 vowels, a question mark, and a comma went to court. They will be sentenced next Friday.

They found a little hole in the wall of the women's soccer team changing rooms. Policemen are looking into it now.

I forgot to turn off the oven yesterday, but it's OK - I just got some Darth Vader cookies. A bit on the dark side.

When you get depressed in the middle of winter, just

chuck some butter from your window. You'll see a butterfly.

My girlfriend bet me I'd never be able to build a car out of spaghetti. She sure looked surprised as I drove pasta.

How to embarrass an archaeologist? You give him a used tampon and ask him to determine which period it came from.

I was picking up my girl. Her dad looked at me very sternly and said, "I want her home by midnight, young man!" - I said, "What do you mean? You already own her home!"

Beethoven: So what up, guys? Are you ready for some serious symphonies? - Excited crowd: YEEEAAAAHHHHH!! - Beethoven: I can't hear you!!!...

I bought shoes from a second hand shop. I think they must've belonged to some junkie though because I've been tripping the whole day.

I have the memory of an elephant. - I very clearly

remember seeing an elephant once in the Chicago zoo.

What's the difference between glue, a tuna and a piano? "No idea." "You could tuna piano, but you couldn't piano a tuna." "Oh. And what's with the glue?" "I knew you'd get stuck there."

Why did Billy throw his pocket watch out of the window? - Because he heard his parents saying that time flies.

A boy ate some coins for fun and his parents took him to the hospital. One hour later the parents asked the nurse how it was going. Apparently, "no change yet."

A guy was taking his girlfriend to prom. Getting ready, he went to a tux rental shop. There was a huge line but he eventually got his tuxedo. He then went to the florist. Again, there was a huge line, but he got the orchid in the end. Then he went to the limo rental place, and there was a big line there too! But he eventually managed to rent one. They got to the prom and danced for a little bit, and then his girlfriend asked for some punch. He went to get it – but there was no punch line.

A bacon sandwich walks into a bar and orders a whiskey. "Sorry," growls the bartender, "we don't serve food here."

I was kind of bored lately so I decided to take up fencing. But the neighbors are threatening to call the police unless I put it down again.

How many psychologists does it take to change a lightbulb? - Well, one, but the lightbulb really has to change itself.

Why didn't the toilet paper go down the water slide like everybody else? Well, he got stuck in the crack.

There were two straw hats on a hanger. One of them said to the other, "Tell you what, you enjoy yourself here for a while longer, I'll go on a-head."

They're building a restaurant on Mars now. They say the food will be great, but they're worried about a lack of atmosphere.

-----

10

901 - 1,000

I saw an offer in a shop – "TV for $4.50 – the volume is stuck on maximum" – It was an offer I simply couldn't turn down.

I don't want to cut my hair! I'm really attached to it! Notice on a shoe repair shop: I'll heel you, I'll save your sole, I'll even gladly dye for you.

Have you heard about this dude who had to have his left leg and left arm amputated after a car crash? -- He's all right now."

Nurse to a doctor: Doctor, here's your list of heart, liver and kidney donors. I already sorted them alphabetically. Doctor: Excellent job...Seriously well organ-ized.

Doctor: You're obese. Patient: For that I definitely want a second opinion. Doctor: You're quite ugly, too.

Do you think that when Han Solo married Princess Leia, she demanded that he change his name to Han Married?

I dig, you dig, she dig, we dig, you dig...the poem may not be beautiful, but it's certainly very deep.

Robert Crinklethumbknut, international tongue-twister champion, made headlines when he got arrested. The rumor is, he's getting a really tough sentence.

I asked my boss if I can come to work a little late today. He said "Dream on." I think that was really nice of him.

I caught some vegans in my basement. I mean, I think they're vegan. All day long, they keep shouting 'lettuce leaf!'

I told my girlfriend to come with me to the gym. Then I stood her up. Hopefully, she'll realize the two of us are not going to work out.

That awkward moment when your friend told you their dog died, and, without thinking, you say, "Oh no, that must have been ruff…"

Vegans believe meat eaters and butchers are gross. But those who sell you fruits and vegetables are grocer.

My boss yelled at me the other day, "You've got to be the worst train driver in history. How many trains did you derail last year?" I said, "Can't say for sure, it's so hard to keep track!"

Daddy somebody's at the door. He's collecting for the district's new indoor swimming pool. Ok, give him a bucket of water then.

A guy goes to a doctor because he's got a strawberry growing out of his chest. The doctor looks and examines and finally says, "Let me give you some cream to put on it."

Daughter: "Mom, can I get a cat or a dog at Christmas, please?" Mom: "No honey, you will be getting turkey, like every Christmas!"

I got my girlfriend a "Get better soon" card. She's not ill or anything, but she could definitely get better.

Two underpants meet for a beer. "Why are you so brown?" asks one. "Don't ask. It was a really crappy week."

A patient bursts into a doctor's office, "Doctor, I believe I'm a deck of cards!" The doctor calmly replies, "Go sit in the waiting room, please, I'll be dealing with you later." A Spanish magician has a grand magical show and at the end he says he will disappear after counting to three. He starts to count, "Un, dos..." Kazaam! He vanished without a tres.

A bear walks into a restaurant and say's "I want a grilllllled..cheese." The waiter says "Whats with the pause?" The bear replies "Whaddya mean, I'M A BEAR."

I went in to a pet shop. I said, "Can I buy a goldfish?" The guy said, "Do you want an aquarium?" I said, "I don't care what star sign it is."

What do you get when you cross a dyslexic, an insomniac, and an agnostic? Someone who lays awake at night wondering if there is a dog.

A pirate walks into a bar with a steering wheel on his pants, a peg leg and a parrot on his shoulder. The bartender says, "Hey, you've got a steering wheel on your pants." The pirate says, "Arrrr, I know. It's driving me nuts."

A man is walking in the desert with his horse and his dog when the dog says, "I can't do this. I need water." The man says, "I didn't know dogs could talk." The horse says, "Me neither!"

A guy goes into a lawyer's office and asks the lawyer: "Excuse me, how much do you charge?" The lawyer responds: "I charge £1,000 to answer three questions." "Bloody hell – That's a bit expensive isn't it?" "Yes. What's your third question?"

What is the resemblance between a green apple and

a red apple? They're both red except for the green one.

I have an EpiPen. My friend gave it to me when he was dying, it seemed very important to him that I have it.

My roommate told me my clothes look gay. I was like, don't be a dick dude; they just came out of the closet.

Never criticize someone until you have walked a mile in their shoes. That way, when you criticize them, you'll be a mile away, and you'll have their shoes.

I couldn't believe that the highway department called my dad a thief. But when I got home, all the signs were there.

If you want to find out who loves you more, stick your wife and dog in the trunk of your car for an hour. When you open the trunk, who is happy to see you?

About a month before he died, my uncle had his

back covered in lard. After that, he went down hill fast.

The first computer dates back to Adam and Eve. It was an Apple with limited memory, just one byte. And then everything crashed.

Doctor, there's a patient on line 1 that says he's invisible "Well, tell him I can't see him right now."

I bought some shoes from a drug dealer. I don't know what he laced them with, but I've been tripping all day.

My girlfriend told me she was leaving me because I keep pretending to be a Transformer. I said, "No, wait! I can change."

I got a new pair of gloves today, but they're both 'lefts' which, on the one hand, is great, but on the other, it's just not right.

My dad died when we couldn't remember his blood type. As he died, he kept insisting for us to "be positive," but it's hard without him.

A cop just knocked on my door and told me that my dogs were chasing people on bikes. My dogs don't even own bikes...

What's the difference of deer nuts and beer nuts? Beer nuts are a $1.75, but deer nut are under a buck.

My girlfriend said, "You act like a detective too much. I want to split up." "Good idea," I replied. "We can cover more ground that way."

What's the difference between a poorly dressed man on a bicycle and a nicely dressed man on a tricycle? A tire.

Did you hear about the guy who got hit in the head with a can of soda? He was lucky it was a soft drink.

I bought a dictionary and when I got home I realized all the pages were blank; I have no words for how angry I am.

Two blondes were driving to Disneyland. The sign said, "Disneyland Left". So they started crying and went home.

Did you hear they banned fans from doing "The Wave" at all sports events? Too many blondes were drowning.

If the right side of the brain controls the left side of the body, then lefties are the only ones in their right mind.

Thieves had broken into my house and stolen everything except my soap, shower gel, towels and deodorant. Dirty Bastards.

Did you hear about the math teacher who's afraid of negative numbers? He will stop at nothing to avoid them.

A teacher asks a student, "Are you ignorant or just apathetic?" The kid answers, "I don't know and I don't care."

It's been raining for 3 days without stopping. My wife is in depression, she is standing and looking through the window. If the rain doesn't stop tomorrow, I'll have to let her in.

A friend of mine tried to annoy me with bird puns,

but I soon realized that toucan play at that game.

I always wanted to marry an Archeologist. The older I would get, the more interested she would become!

My psychiatrist said I was pre-occupied with the vengeance I told him "oh yeah we'll see about that!"

I recently got a new Korean mechanic but it's hard to understand him - he speaks with a Hyundai Accent!

I bought a box of condoms earlier today. The cashier asked if I'd like a bag. I said "nah, I'll just turn the lights off."

My grandfather tried to warn them about the Titanic. He screamed and shouted about the iceberg and how the ship was going to sink, but all they did was throw him out of the theater.

I'm changing my name to 'Benefits' on Facebook. Next time someone adds me, It will say "you are now friends with Benefits."

I ran out of poker chips so used dry fruits for playing

instead. People went nuts when they saw me raisin the stakes.

Hackers brought down my online business but I managed to keep the website address and that's domain thing.

A bus station is where a bus stops. A train station is where a train stops. On my desk, I have a work station..

Confucius say, man who runs behind car will get exhausted, but man who runs in front of car will get tired.

I finally realized my parents favored my twin brother. It hit me when they asked me to blow up balloons for his surprise birthday party.

Can a kangaroo jump higher than the Empire State Building? Of course. The Empire State Building can't jump.

The nurse at the sperm bank asked me if I'd like to masturbate in the cup. I said, "Well, I'm pretty good, but I don't think I'm ready to compete just yet."

The recipe said "Set the oven to 180 degrees" so I did, but now I can't open it because the door faces the wall.

My buddy set me up on a blind date & said, "Heads up, she's expecting a baby." Felt like an idiot sitting in the bar wearing just a diaper.

My girlfriend tried to make me have sex on the hood of her Honda Civic. I refused. If I'm going to have sex, it's going to be on my own Accord.

Why did Martin Luther King Jr. boycott laundry detergent? Because it told him to keep his whites and colors separate.

The therapist asked my wife why she wanted to end our marriage. She said she hated all the constant Star Wars puns. I look at the therapist and said, "Divorce is strong with this one!"

Just saw a heavyset man carrying loads of weapons, even had one hanging out of his backside... it was big arse 'n' all.

A guy goes to a club; the bouncer stops him. "No tie, no entry." He walks back to his car to find a tie. All he found were jumper cables so he puts them around his neck like a tie. He goes back and says "How's this?" The bouncer says "I'll let you in, but don't start anything."

My girlfriend asked me to pass her the Chapstick and I accidentally passed her the Glue Stick! She still hasn't talked to me!

Grandma's been staring through the window ever since it started to snow. If it gets any worse I'll have to let her in.

To the women who say "Men are only interested in one thing." Have you ever considered being more interesting?

My landlord says he needs to come talk to me about how high my heating bill is. I told him, "My door is always open".

One time somebody said if I was an element, I'd be copper. Then someone else told me I'm tellurium. Does that mean I'm CuTe?

Girl, are you a modern day savings account because I keep investing money in you but I'm not getting much interest.

I wear two pairs of pants when I go golfing. People always ask me why I do. I say, "I wear two pants when's I golf just in case I get a hole-in-one.

I turned on the light to wake up my kids. My 2-year-old turned it off and went back to bed. She used to be the family alarm clock. Now she's the snooze button.

Did you know that if you hold your ear up to a strangers leg you can actually hear them say "what the fuck are you doing?

If 2 guys are having sex and the house catches on fire. Who gets out first, the guy on top or the guy on the bottom? The guy on the bottom cause he's already got his shit packed.

I own a pencil that used to be owned by William Shakespeare, but he chewed it a lot. Now I can't tell if it's 2B or not 2B.

I have won first place in this Halloween costume contest 16 years in a row. This year I am dressed as a hotdog. I'm on a roll.

I cooked Pancakes this morning. I was thrilled but my kids weren't. Apparently, he was their favorite rabbit.

Today, my son asked "Can I have a book mark?" and I burst into tears. 11 years old and he still doesn't know my name is Brian.

-----

3 men are stranded in a boat with 4 cigarettes and no way to light them. So they toss the 4th cigarette overboard, which makes the whole boat a cigarette lighter.

My cross-eyed wife and I just got a divorce. We didn't see eye to eye. I also found out she was seeing someone on the side.

I trapped a couple of vegans in my basement. At least I think they're vegan. They keep shouting 'lettuce leaf!'

I sat next to a man on the park bench. He had 9 watches on one wrist and 5 in the other. I said man "you sure do have a lot of time on your hands."

I work out almost every day. Friday I almost worked out, Saturday I almost worked out, Sunday I almost worked out...

Hitting birds is illegal and you get a big fine, I learned this when I kicked a pelican... I ended up footing a massive bill.

The artist thought his favourite paint had been stolen, but it was just a pigment of his imagination.

If you ever get cold, just stand in the corner of a room for a while. They're normally around 90 degrees.

What does a disappointed mama turkey tell her kids? If your father were to see you now, he would be turning over in his gravy!

Mom: If a boy touches your boobs say "don't" and if he touches your pussy say "stop"? Girl: But mom, he touched both so I said "don't stop".

Some species of frog can jump higher than a 3-story office building. It's because of their immensely powerful hind legs, and the fact that office buildings cannot jump.

Here's a step by step guide to walking up the stairs, step 1) Right foot, step 2) Left foot, step 3) Right foot...

The other day I was singing in the shower, and I got soap in my mouth. Guess what happened then? It became a soap opera.

I'm trying to finish writing a script for a porno movie, but there are just too many holes in the plot.

Lightning Source UK Ltd.
Milton Keynes UK
UKHW012303011220
374454UK00002B/331